LABRADORS

FRANK WARNER HILL is acknowledged as being among the foremost gundog experts in Great Britain today. He has written here a lucid survey of the care and training of the Labrador from the puppy to the adult dog stage. Any newcomer to the breed, wishing to acquire a Labrador, will find no better book to guide him than this.

General Editor: CHRISTINA FOYLE

LABRADORS

BY

F. WARNER HILL

FOYLES HANDBOOKS
LONDON

Reprinted 1972
© W. & G. Foyle Ltd. 1966
Revised edition 1973
Reprinted 1974
Reprinted 1975

ISBN 0 7071 0329 0

Printed and bound in Great Britain by
REDWOOD BURN LIMITED
Trowbridge & Esher

CONTENTS

LIST OF ILLUSTRATIONS

FOREWORD

MR. WARNER HILL has very kindly asked me to write a Foreword to his book on the Labrador Retriever. Needless to say I am delighted to do so, for Mr. Warner Hill has had a vast experience of breeding, showing and judging gundogs.

I was the original Honorary Secretary of the Labrador Retriever Club, an office I still hold (the club was founded in 1916) and I am now, and have been since 1933, Chairman of the Club. Like Mr. Warner Hill, I have the true interest of the breed at heart, and I was delighted that at our 1958 Championship Show Mr. Warner Hill received a record entry. At Field Trials he is an equally popular and impartial judge; under these happy conditions I can only wish great success to the book he has written which I know will be of infinite value to novices and old hands. I hope the book will have the success it deserves—I am sure it will!

LORNA HOWE
(Countess Howe)
Chairman, Labrador Retriever Club

INTRODUCTION

INVITED to write a short book on this famous gun dog breed I turned up the map of the continent of North America to gain a more intimate knowledge on the lie of the land. Starting at the famous Bay of Chesapeake, famed in song and story, from which the only true sporting gun dog of the United States takes its name, the Chesapeake Bay Retriever, we move up the coast until we come to Newfoundland. Here, of course, everyone is aware is the home of that great long-coated black dog, subject of famous paintings by Landseer. Occasionally these dogs come black and white, in contrast to the normal black-coated dogs, and are actually called Landseers. Travelling north again we come to the Labrador Peninsula, approaching the northern coast of Canada, where one can look straight across towards the Greenland coast.

This is wild and rugged coastland where a hardy race of people dwell who largely depend for their livelihood on fishing, and to some extent on the killing of wild fowl, and they developed a great dog for general utility purposes in this bleak country. There are several theories as to how this breed returned or first arrived in England, many of them considerably open to suspicion. But the fact remains that the Labradors did come over here and appealed greatly to gun dog people generally. Over the years they have gradually supplanted the Curly-coated Retriever, and the Flat-coated Retriever, the most popular breeds before the Labrador put in an appearance.

Living in the county of Dorset, I find a number of local sportsmen stoutly maintain that Labrador Retrievers were first introduced into England by trading seamen who brought them over from Labrador and landed in Poole Harbour. This idea has many supporters outside the county and could very well be the true story behind the beginning of the breed in this country. It has been found, however, that many recorders of breed history have differed widely on what constitutes a Labrador Retriever. The descriptions they offer bear little relation one to the other,

11

and it is obvious to me that many of the dogs brought into this country were not the pure Labrador. Throughout the years we have found that the true Labrador breeds exactly to type for generation after generation, decade after decade, till the present day finds the Labrador to be the top retriever breed of England with thousands of dogs all of the same type, the same character, and the same natural aptitude for work that first attracted the interest of our sporting forebears.

It must be admitted that certain breeders have in the last twenty or thirty years indulged in some rather indiscriminate crossing which has produced fast dogs and quick retrievers, and these bear little resemblance to the original breed. These dogs appear mostly in competition at field trials, and are used and bred largely by people who have little interest in the show bench or the physical beauty of the breed. Chief breed supporters from the olden days all maintain, and I believe rightly so, that very little has been gained by this type of breeding; perhaps a little more speed, but then I doubt if they have been able to increase their scenting powers to keep pace. All that has been achieved then is a speedy dog which is inclined to overrun his game if the scent is not particularly good. Of course, one finds a great many very typical Labradors competing and winning at trials, and many of these dogs also go on to win championships on the show bench and become that greatest and most desirable dog, the dual champion, field trial and show bench champion.

Labradors have always commanded the highest patronage and all the great sporting estates of this country have kept them at some time or another, and today the Labrador Retriever Club finds itself in a stronger position than ever, and its members are fortunate in securing Her Majesty The Queen as their Patron.

Labradors have, for a great many years, been included in the Royal Kennels at Sandringham, and at various shows in the eastern counties I have had the honour, before the war particularly, of judging exhibits owned by three different Kings of England. Actually the head of this section of the estate in pre-war days, Mr. Bland, was a great personal friend of our family, and when the royal dogs were exhibited outside the immediate environs of their home, Mr. Bland always accompanied them. The last time I had the honour of competing against a Labrador Retriever from Sandringham was in Lancashire in the pre-war days. One of our great all-round judges in England put the King's Labrador the best exhibit of all breeds in the show and I am very proud to be the possessor of the cup for the best opposite sex of all breeds in the show. My exhibit on this occasion being an English Springer Spaniel, Champion Beauchief Bonetta.

In this country at the present time there are 107 individual breeds of dog acknowledged by the Kennel Club and included in their Register of Breeds. Top of the lot at the moment are the Miniature Poodles which, in 1951, had 3,984 registrations and in 1959 totalled 21,239 registrations, an unprecedented increase for any breed in canine history. Second come the highly popular Pembroke Corgis. These are the favourite dogs of the Royal Family today and from 4,595 registrations in 1951 they have increased to 8,580 at the present time. Third place in the list of registrations goes to the Alsatians which have maintained their registrations steadily for many years. Next come the Boxers which numbered 4,464 registrations in 1951 and today number 6,979. Fifth we have the Cocker Spaniels, and here alas there has been a considerable decline. In 1951 the registrations were 12,871 but today little more than half that number maintains, 6,515. This is a sad story and a sign of the changing of the times. No doubt this breed and all spaniel breeds were very adversely affected when myxomatosis cleared out the rabbit population of these islands, robbing the countrymen of a very cheap form of sport and many a good dinner for the working classes. Sixth in the list we have the top of the toy dog section, the Pekingese. From 5,466 registrations in 1951 there has been a slight decline to 5,195 but they are maintaining quite steadily over this period their standing in the list of breeds. Seventh—and seventh out of 107 breeds you must admit is a very high position indeed—come our Labrador Retrievers which in 1951 achieved 3,859 registrations, suffered a slight decline, recovered again in 1956 until in 1958 we find them with 4,672 registrations.

These figures I have given you, of course, are merely comparative. They show the number of dogs registered with the Kennel

Club each year in their respective breed, but have no bearing on the actual number of that breed alive in the country at that particular time. What it means is practically that in each of these breeds the numbers I have given you are the youngsters that have been registered this year, and just to give you some indication of the magnitude of the dog-breeding industry in this country I might mention that the total registrations of all breeds for 1958 total 115,678. I think you will agree that these figures, without particular detailed reference, are quite impressive as far as the Labrador Retrievers are concerned, particularly when I might say their chief contestants in the popularity poll, the Golden Retrievers, numbered in 1951, 2,128 registrations and in 1958, 2,222. Where the Goldens have more than maintained their popularity, the Labradors have considerably increased theirs.

Here is proof, if proof be needed, of the claims for the Labrador Retriever. To start with one or two casual, maybe accidental, importations, and throughout the years to increase and maintain type, until we find so many distributed all over the country to the extent I have shown in these foregoing statistics, speaks well for the general appeal of this wonderful breed.

At the time of writing, news of the breed comes from Australia. Judging all breeds at their Centenary Show at Melbourne some years ago—250 dogs per day for eight days—I found only a few Labradors, but at their most recent show they have jumped to one of the best breeds. Good news also comes from America where again they are gaining ground rapidly.

CHAPTER 1

WHAT IS A LABRADOR?

THIS book does not pretend to be a scientific treatise for the expert breeder. I hope to give the general outline, and to those who have not yet owned a gun dog, some little insight into the charm, the utility and the general attractiveness of this very lovable breed.

The Labrador is principally referred to in two colours—the Black Labrador and the Yellow Labrador, there being just odd specimens Chocolate in colour. I'm afraid the second is not a very attractive name—no one likes to be called yellow—but it has to be, for, there are strong contenders on the show bench and in work in the shooting field, a special breed called the Golden Retrievers. These are in the main golden in colour, and thus rightfully called Golden Retrievers. To avoid confusion, however, golden coloured Labradors could not carry the name, and so we have to be content with the Black Labrador and Yellow Labrador—'yellow', of course, embracing any colour from dark red to very light cream.

In the early days the blacks were predominant, both at the field trials and particularly on the show bench, to such an extent that admirers of the Yellow Labradors banded together, formed a special club, and by using their influence were able to obtain special classes for Yellow Labradors only at the big championship shows. However, by selective breeding and, of course, by mating blacks with reds, which is a perfectly legitimate thing to do, the standard of the Yellow Labrador gradually improved until today they need no protection from the Black Labradors, either at work, on the show bench, or in field trial competition. In fact, although we still separate the colours at the big shows, it is not really necessary any longer.

As far as general utility and work is concerned, there is

nothing to choose between a black and a yellow, and if you are interested in the breed I think it can be left to personal preference as to choice of colour. Some say the yellows are not quite so easy to see in cover, but when a retriever is working in thick cover, retrieving game, there should be no danger of his being shot, for it is not considered etiquette to continue firing when the dogs are picking up.

Talking of gun dogs generally one always likes to feel that sometimes they are able to indulge in the work for which they were originally bred, but it is realized today that many cannot possibly hope to give their dogs this opportunity. However, Labradors are most adaptable, they make very fine house dogs and companions, and are extremely good and safe with children. There is, too, another great use for this breed which since the last war has given pleasure and interest in an otherwise deadly world, and that is for blind people. The Labrador makes a first-class guide dog, and I frequently see them being trained for this type of work by the trainers at the Exeter Centre; I have often spoken to them regarding the work of these dogs and they say the Labrador Retriever bitch is most adaptable, and makes a faithful guard, companion and friend to a blind person.

So whether you take an interest in shooting or not, it is clear that a Labrador can make a very fine companion and a guard of your house, while you can train him to do all manner of things, fetching and carrying generally. This will give him at least some interest in exercising his natural ability.

The ultimate success of the Labrador breed is attributed greatly to those original patrons, such as the Honourable A. Holland-Hibbert, in 1884, who later became Lord Knutsford, and owned the Munden Prefix in Hertfordshire. In Scotland, the Duke of Buccleuch (1806-84) had many notable dogs and created a pioneer kennel in the breed; and later on we also find that Lord Malmsbury took a considerable interest in them.

Above all, however, stands Lorna, Countess Howe, to whom the whole of the Labrador world of today owes a deep debt of gratitude for her loyalty to the breed and her devoted work in its welfare. Behind her famous kennel stands that great sire, dual champion Banchory Bolo, whose head we reproduce on the cover of this book.

There is a romantic story attached to this dog's rise to fame. I am afraid there have been many erroneous impressions created by various writers, and I have not read an entirely true version in any book on the breed. I consider myself greatly privileged to be able to give you the true story of this foundation dog in the Labrador breed, as written to me personally by Lady Howe.

Her Ladyship, at the turn of the century, owned a Labrador called Scandal, who only sired one litter of which twelve out of thirteen were bitches with only one dog. Unhappily Scandal died of canine typhus contracted through drinking stagnant water, before producing any more litters. This single dog from the big litter I have mentioned, changed hands once or twice, for no one could master him—he was untrainable and he was unbiddable. Finally, Lady Howe was so determined that she should have a descendant of her first Labrador, that she acquired the dog Bolo.

Living in those days at Walcot, Bolo was one day being exercised in the kennel yard, when at nothing more than the crack of a whip he was gone. Search was made for him without avail. The door to the house was left open and her Ladyship retired to bed at one a.m. leaving her door open and his basket readily available. Wakening at six a.m., there was Bolo stretched out in his basket; he presented a very sorry picture with two stab wounds in the chest, the breast bone bared, and stomach injuries as well. It was found that clearing the precincts of the buildings he had jumped a 6 ft. 6 in. iron gate with spiked top and had become impaled. He had managed to drag himself free and then vanished into the country.

Those who saw him said immediately that he should be destroyed, but not so his owner. Her veterinary surgeon, living eight miles away at Craven Arms, was known to be out, so calling in a kennelman, Bowes, Lady Howe personally put in over twenty stitches to close up his wounds.

'He just kept perfectly quiet', says Lady Howe in her letter, 'though I must have hurt him, as besides the stitching I put two tubes in to drain the deep wounds. All went well till a few days later he heard shooting near the house. I was trying to get a puppy out of some thick brambles when I heard 'crash! bang!' and out came old Bolo with the bird, but he had torn most of the stitches out. So I had to stitch the poor old man up and never a murmur or movement came from him. This was in 1919, and in 1923 both he and his son Corby were both very ill and the vet thought they had been poisoned. Both had very bad internal hae-morrhages, the veterinary surgeon looked after Corby and I nursed Bolo. They were both in London with me. That was the only illness we ever had, and he was a dual champion then. Anyway, I shall never have a dog like him.'

That is the story of the greatest dog in the breed in his day and possibly the greatest dog the breed has ever known. Originally described as a bad dog, but with good treatment he became one of the greatest companion dogs and greatest working dogs. Naturally a very good looking dog, he became champion both in the field and on the bench, and throughout his life was the firm companion of Lady Howe.

I can almost guarantee that if you purchase a Labrador with an extended pedigree, you will find that the probable great-great-great-grandfather of your puppy is Dual Champion Banchory Bolo.

Talking of pillars of the breed, I might mention just one more great dog, and this was also owned by Lady Howe and named Bramshaw Bob. This dog was a great worker, and practically unbeatable on the show bench. He became a champion in three successive shows; the first time he was exhibited at Crufts great international dog show in 1932, he was judged best of all breeds in the show and he repeated this performance in 1933, quite an exceptional thing for any dog to achieve.

Great, however, as Bramshaw Bob was in his day, nothing can supplant champion Bolo in the affections of his mistress. Lady Howe, who has recently written an extensive work on the breed, has actually been asked to write a complete history of this individual dog, which, I understand, is nearing completion. Lady Howe described him to me as in her opinion the finest Labrador that was ever bred and the one that did most good for the breed.

By now you will no doubt realize what a wonderful breed of

dog we are writing about. His great capacity for loyalty, companionship and ever-ready willingness to please commends him to all lovers of the breed, and it has been said with considerable truth that once a Labrador owner, always a Labrador owner.

DOGS AT WAR

It is generally known that dogs played a great part in the past war in guarding airfields and acting as guard dogs generally on shore establishments. It is not, however, generally known what a great part they played in the fall of Cassino; and among the dogs employed in Italy some were Labrador Retrievers. The story shortly is this, as told to me by the Principal of the War Dogs School.

Our troops were suffering so many losses in their patrols trying to establish a sound roadway to Cassino for the main body and, of course, the mechanized vehicles, that eventually appeal was made to this friend of mine who went out to Italy and there supervised the work of dogs in scenting out the minefields which had been heavily laid all round the castle. The dogs had an uncanny aptitude for discovering hidden mines, and as they progressed so the mine recovery people cleared the road to Cassino. It was largely through the efforts of these dogs that the fortress was finally invested. This, surely, is a great testimonial to dogs generally and Labradors in particular.

You will probably be interested in the following story which appeared in one of the daily papers. It was entitled DEMOB, NOT DEATH FOR DARK—'Dark, the old war-dog (he's an eight-year-old Labrador in service in bandit-infested Malaya) is not to be put down. He's to be demobbed. But it has taken a six-month intensive campaign to do it, involving captains, majors and a brigadier.

'Memos and minutes in triplicate, filled in- and out-trays; telephone calls buzzed incessantly (and heatedly); signals flashed between War Office and Malaya before the brass-hats agreed that Dark is "surplus to operational requirements."

'This week Dark is expected to leave Kluang Johore, for a port of embarkation for the UK and reunion with his devoted master, ex-Corporal Howard Robson, of Carlisle. The cost: £100.

'Robson and Dark were together on Howard's National Service with the Royal Army Veterinary Corps attached to the 2-7th Ghurka Rifles in the jungle.'

Here again is romantic proof—if proof be needed—of the great partnership that can be created between a man and his dog and particularly between a man and his Labrador.

CHAPTER 2

THE STANDARD OF THE BREED

THE Kennel Club, governing body of the dog world, have, in consultation with breed clubs, created standards for each of the breeds. They also give a description and sometimes heights and weight limits. The standard is the equivalent of bogie score at a game of golf. You should study the standard carefully and then look at your dog and see how far and in what points he fails so far as the standard is concerned and, should it be a bitch, when it comes to breeding, you will have some idea, or a better idea, of which dog to use to try and correct these faults in your puppies. The following is the official standard of the Labrador as published by the Kennel Club.

GENERAL APPEARANCE—The general appearance of the Labrador should be that of a strongly-built, short-coupled, very active dog, broad in the skull, broad and deep through the chest and ribs, broad and strong over the loins and hindquarters. The coat close, short with dense undercoat and free from feather. The dog must move neither too wide nor too close in front or behind, he must stand and move true all round on legs and feet.

HEAD AND SKULL—The skull should be broad with a pronounced stop so that the skull is not in a straight line with the nose. The head should be clean cut without fleshy cheeks. The jaws should be medium length and powerful and free from snipiness. The nose wide and the nostrils well developed.

EYES—The eyes of medium size expressing intelligence and good temper, should be brown or hazel.

EARS—Should not be large and heavy and should hang close to the head, and set rather far back.

MOUTH—Teeth should be sound and strong. The lower teeth just behind but touching the upper.

NECK—Should be clean, strong and powerful and set into well placed shoulders.

FOREQUARTERS—The shoulders should be long and sloping. The forelegs well boned and straight from the shoulder to the ground when viewed from either the front or side. The dog must move neither too wide nor too close in front.

BODY—The chest must be of good width and depth with well-sprung ribs. The back should be short-coupled.

HINDQUARTERS—The loins must be wide and strong with well-turned stifles; hindquarters well developed and not sloping to the tail. The hocks should be slightly bent and the dog must neither be cow-hocked nor move too wide or too close behind.

FEET—Should be round and compact with well-arched toes and well-developed pads.

TAIL—The tail is a distinctive feature of the breed; it should be very thick towards the base, gradually tapering towards the tip, of medium length and practically free from any feathering, but clothed thickly all round with the Labrador's short, thick, dense coat, thus giving that peculiar 'rounded' appearance which has been described as the 'Otter' tail. The tail may be carried gaily, but should not curl over the back.

COAT—The coat is another distinctive feature of the breed, it should be short and dense and without wave with a weather-resisting undercoat and should give a fairly hard feeling to the hand.

COLOUR—The colour is generally black, chocolate or yellow —which may vary from fox-red to cream—free from any white markings. A small white spot on the chest is allowable, the coat should be of a whole colour and not of a flecked appearance.

WEIGHT AND SIZE—Desired height for Dogs, 22-22½ inches: Bitches, 21½-22 inches.

FAULTS—Under or overshot mouth; no undercoat; bad action; feathering; snipiness on the head; large or heavy ears; cow-hocked; tail curled over back.

CHAPTER 3

GREAT LABRADORS OF PAST AND PRESENT

IN THE introduction to this book I did specifically say it was not supposed to be a scientific treatise on the production of the perfect Labrador. It is written in the simplest manner I can achieve to interest particularly the novice owner and the prospective Labrador owner. Each of the chapters which sub-divide this book could provide a subject for a whole book on its own, therefore you must realize that in simplifying I have had to condense a great deal, but as I say, with so many clubs available and so many helpful people about, you can get that direct personal advice which is so much more satisfying than anything you merely read.

You will notice with every illustration of a top show dog or worker pictured in the following pages, I give you details of the wins or the breeding of the animal, together with its pedigree, and if you compare one with another you will see really how closely linked are our top dogs. These examples I have chosen with the greatest care, and the more you study both the pictures and pedigrees the more you will appreciate the art of pedigree dog breeding.

CHAMPION LANDYKE VELOUR

(Property of the late J. Hart, J.P., Granby Farm, Knipton, Grantham, Lincs, and his son Mr. J. Keith Hart.)

As OUR illustration shows (p. 25) Velour proved to be one of the greatest yellow bitches the breed has known. For a time she was in the Kennel of Lady Howe, and later returned to her home kennel, and the last time I judged her was the National Show at

Birmingham when she was handled by Mr. Keith Hart, when it was regretted that the failing health of his father prevented him seeing her win, in extremely good company, her Best of Breed award. Immediately after the Show Lady Howe wrote to me concerning the Labradors exhibited there. 'Some were I should think three parts Flatcoats and some black Whippets. This mania for speed is telling its tale. Velour is a real old Labrador and so is your reserve winner'. (Ch. Corsican Quest owned by Colonel and Mrs. Venn of the Manor House, Beeston, Notts., great breeders and supporters also of Field Trials). Later Lady Howe said 'Congratulations on your article on Labradors; I am pleased that some one at long last is taking up the cause of the correct-type Labrador and you were perfectly right in classing Velour as a first class specimen of this type, and you are at liberty to say so'.

Later, forthright Lady Howe, who puts the welfare of Labradors before any other consideration, also said 'Unfortunately some [and by this she means only a proportion for we still have fine typical specimens successfully competing] of the Labradors running at Field Trials today bear more resemblance to Whippets than they do to the true type of Labrador, yet the real old Labrador used to win on the Bench and in the Field, and I do not think so much game was left on the ground at field trials in the old days as is left today, when the dogs which gallop at full speed (and are subservient to their handlers' signals and whistles and not their noses) seem to be sought out for high awards. I did not see the bitches judged at Birmingham, but I am most certainly well acquainted with the bitch Certificate winner which was also best of breed. She is most certainly a true Labrador in type, character, coat, expression and tail, and has plenty of bone and substance.' (Now I want you novice owners and breeders to particularly note what comes next) 'If breeders will stick to her type they will not go wrong, but if this Whippety type goes much further then we shall soon see exhibits being carried into the ring if their handlers feel so inclined. Certainly no one in their right senses would wish to carry Landyke Velour far!' Just a note in passing. Lady Howe referred to Ch. Corsican Quest as reserve certificate winner to Velour. She was exactly the same age, and she won the

CH. LANDYKE VELOUR

PEDIGREE OF CHAMPION LANDYKE VELOUR

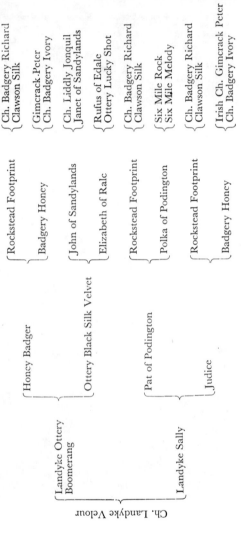

Ch. Landyke Velour

Landyke Ottery Boomerang

   Honey Badger

      Rockstead Footprint
          Ch. Badgery Richard
          Clawson Silk

      Badgery Honey
          Gimcrack-Peter
          Ch. Badgery Ivory

   Ottery Black Silk Velvet

      John of Sandylands
          Ch. Liddly Jonquil
          Janet of Sandylands

      Elizabeth of Ralc
          Rufus of Edale
          Ottery Lucky Shot

Landyke Sally

   Pat of Podington

      Rockstead Footprint
          Ch. Badgery Richard
          Clawson Silk

      Polka of Podington
          Six Mile Rock
          Six Mile Melody

   Judice

      Rockstead Footprint
          Ch. Badgery Richard
          Clawson Silk

      Badgery Honey
          Irish Ch. Gimcrack Peter
          Ch. Badgery Ivory

class for Labradors which had run at Field Trials and obtained at least a certificate of merit on their work.

Both these were bitches of excellent substance with big bodies, features of the breed, and far removed from the small lightly built animals which deviate from the correct type.

I would suggest you all study the pedigree of Ch. Landyke Velour, where three lines of Champion Badgery Richard and two lines of Champion Badgery Ivory are finally merged in this bitch. These two Champions were great winners in the pre-war era.

Of considerable significance are the many judges who have awarded Velour Challenge Certificates. They, in addition to her National Show win, include Mr. J. V. Browne who gave her a certificate whilst in the ownership of Lady Howe, and after her return to the Landyke Kennel she won under Mr. H. A. Saunders at the Midland Club Show (Mr Saunders is owner of the famous Liddly Kennel). She won also at the Ladies Kennel Association Ch. Show in London, this under another great breeder and judge Mr. Bob Paton who had an entry of 587 Labradors in the 1959 Crufts where he made Ch. Ruler of Blaircourt Best of Breed (see page 49). She also won Certificates under Mr. Grant Cairns (joint owner of Ch. Ruler), Mr. H. Taylor (joint owner of Ch. Whatstandwell Ballyduff Robin), while Lady Howe herself has also put her to the top. Several other breeder-judges have awarded her Challenge Certificates thereby confirming all the claims made for her as the correct type of Labrador.

DUAL CHAMPION BRAMSHAW BOB

(Owner: Lorna, Countess Howe, Hawkridge House, Hermitage, Newbury, Berks.)

THIS GREATEST of all dual champions was a field trial winner for Sir George Thursby prior to him joining the Banchory Kennel in December 1931. I well remember the start of this dog's career with Lady Howe, for I, too had brought an English Springer

DUAL CHAMPION BRAMSHAW BOB

over from Ireland as an outcross for my own strain—in fact I called him Beauchief Outcross—and we both brought our new dogs out at Crufts, in 1932. My own dog was not quite ready and only stood third for the Championship, but Bob in fine form won his six classes, was best of breed, and finally best exhibit in show all breeds, and didn't the gundog folk and the many keepers present give owner and dog an ovation. They appreciated such a great win with a proved working dog. On to the Edinburgh Ch. Show where again Bob was best all breeds in show (my Springer, improving in condition, moved up to Reserve for the Certificate); and then came Manchester, and again Bob won the Championship and again Best exhibit all breeds, a great triple success. Yes, I had my bit of glory at Manchester too—for my dog beat a good entry to win his first Challenge Certificate, and he too became a Champion later that year. Bob, however, went on to the field trials and soon became a dual champion, and in 1933 he again won best all breeds at Crufts, an honour he was to win at twelve other Championship Shows. His sire, Ch. Ingleston Ben, was runner up to Bob at Crufts in the breed in 1932. Ch. Ingleston Ben was also sire of Lady Howe's Ch. Cheverells Ben of Banchory, which in turn was best in show all breeds at Crufts in 1938. Dual Ch. Bramshaw Bob shares with Dual Champion Banchory Bolo the highest honours and an equal position in the regard of their owner, for they were, with one or two other famous dogs, given complete freedom of the house, and as Lady Howe said to me, 'They never abused their privileges'.

CHAMPION ZELSTONE LEAP YEAR LASS

(Owner Mrs. M. Radcliffe, Owermoigne Moor, Dorchester.)

CHAMPION ZELSTONE LEAP YEAR LASS is a yellow bitch, seven years old, winner of three Challenge Certificates and five Reserve Certificates. She was Best bitch at the Yellow Labrador Club's Open Show in 1955, Best in Show the next year, and again Best bitch in 1958—a great record.

CH. ZELSTONE LEAP YEAR LASS

PEDIGREE OF CHAMPION ZELSTONE LEAP YEAR LASS

Ch. Zelstone Leap Year Lass

- Braedrop Bruce
  - Dual Ch. Staindrop Saighdear
    - Glenhead Jimmy
      - Ch. Kimpurnie Kam Knappies Lass
    - Our Lil
      - F.T. Ch. Glenravel Nimrod Glenravel Glynter
  - F.T. Ch. Braeroy Fudge
    - Banchory Jack
      - Ch. Kimpurnie Kam Dunkeld Duchess
    - Braeroy Chips
      - Braeroy Duke Braeroy Mitie
- F.T. Ch. Zelstone Dartu
  - Durley Bracken
    - Thatchu
      - Toi of Whitmore Drinkstone Stella
    - Liddly Ouzel
      - Liddly Blackcock Judy of Rook
  - Glenmorag Parella of Podington
    - Neptune of Hinwick
      - F.T. Ch. Hawkesbury Jupiter Manor
    - Polka of Podington
      - Six Mile Rock Six Mile Melody

31

A wonderful worker herself, she is a Field Trial winner and the dam of a Field Trial Champion, Zelstone Moss, who has now been mated to Field Trial Champion Galleywood Shot, winner of the Retriever Championship in 1957 and 1958, illustrated on page 37. This is an example of constructive dual purpose breeding, and the pedigrees of these two Labradors should be studied together.

CHAMPION WHATSTANDWELL BALLYDUFF ROBIN

(Property of Mr. and Mrs. H. Taylor, Chase Cliffe, Whatstandwell. Bred by H. J. Easthaugh.)

HERE WE give you an excellent picture (p. 33) of a truly great black dog of the post-war era. He is out of a Champion, is a Champion, and sired a Champion, is a very handsome dog and a brilliant worker with several trial awards to his credit. He has won five Challenge Certificates and five Reserve Certificates. One of his best wins was under Lady Howe at the Labrador Retriever Club's Show of 1954, when she reported 'Ch. Whatstandwell Ballyduff Robin won the Field Trial Class. He is a grand Labrador; his head is a study and reminds one of the late Ch. Withington Ben'. At the same show Robin's famous homebred daughter, Champion Rowena (who was best Labrador at Crufts 1952) was winner of the Challenge Certificate and Best of Breed. Of her, Lady Howe said 'She is indeed a beautiful Labrador'. Robin has proved in addition to his inherent merit one of the greatest sires the breed has known. One year at Paignton Ch. Show, Robin and his progeny, were the top four best dogs and bitches while at the Labrador Club Show three of the top four winners were allied to him. In addition to siring Champion Rowena there is also Ch. Roberta of Coohoy, Ch. Romantic of Coohoy (Best bitch at Crufts 1959) and Whatstandwell Venus who only needs to qualify at Trials to claim the Champion title. Other big winners include Wendover Jonah and Jessie and their litter brother who is winning certificates abroad. These

CH. WHATSTANDWELL BALLYDUFF ROBIN

PEDIGREE OF CH. WHATSTANDWELL BALLYDUFF ROBIN

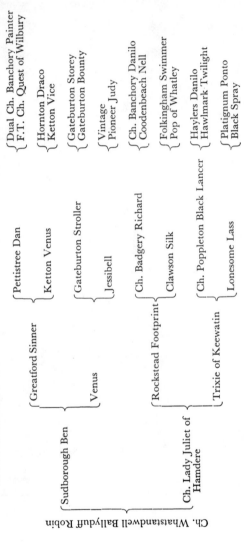

Ch. Whatstandwell Ballyduff Robin

Sudborough Ben

Ch. Lady Juliet of Hamdere

Greatford Sinner

Venus

Rockstead Footprint

Trixie of Keewatin

Pettistree Dan

Ketton Venus

Gateburton Stroller

Jessibell

Ch. Badgery Richard

Clawson Silk

Ch. Poppleton Black Lancer

Lonesome Lass

Dual Ch. Banchory Painter
F.T. Ch. Quest of Wilbury

Hornton Draco
Ketton Vice

Gateburton Storey
Gateburton Bounty

Vintage
Pioneer Judy

Ch. Banchory Danilo
Coodenbeach Nell

Folkingham Swimmer
Pop of Whatley

Haylers Danilo
Hawlmark Twilight

Platignum Ponto
Black Spray

34

were bred in the famous kennel of Mr. and Mrs. L. C. James at Northampton.

Some people would have you believe that dog owners and breeders were lacking in sentiment. Not a bit of it. I am unashamedly publishing part of a letter concerning Robin I have received from Mrs. Taylor who is Hon. Secretary of the Midland Labrador Retriever Club. She says: 'He has really been a *wonder* dog. Just at the height of his working career when we were approaching the F. T. season, full of confidence, he was suddenly stricken with what must have been closely akin to polio. He was out shooting one day, and *completely* paralysed the next, even to his clenched teeth and jaws. After constant nursing day and night he showed improvement after three weeks, and at eight weeks had to learn to walk. But we won, and he made 100% recovery—I would and could not however attempt to run him at F. Trials—(he was entered for six Open Stakes)!—as he had become completely spoilt and it would have meant strict training to get implicit obedience as before, so then we launched him into his brilliant show career. We could have shown him up to being 12 years of age, he was fit enough, but Lady Howe begged us to retire him from shows whilst at the peak of his show career. She maintained he was far too good to be beaten! Now the poor old boy is almost at 'the end of the road!' He has developed heart trouble and a bad cough and he is just hanging on. I'm afraid it can't be for long. His thirteenth birthday should be in June (1959). He's been such a knowledgeable dog and a *real character*, pushing his head under anyone's arm in order to get affection.'

Were you still hesitating about 'going in for Labradors?' Surely the foregoing must convince you.

FIELD TRIAL CHAMPION
GALLEYWOOD SHOT

(Owned by Mr. W. Lawrence Taylor, Galleywood, Chelmsford, Essex.)

THIS ATTRACTIVE picture of Galleywood Shot conveys to the full

PEDIGREE OF FIELD TRIAL CHAMPION GALLEYWOOD SHOT

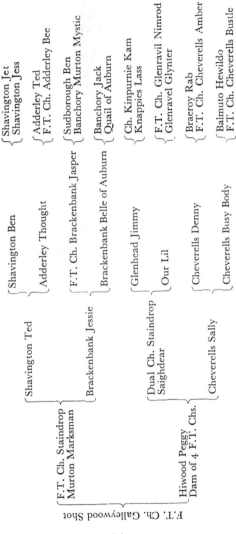

F.T. Ch. Galleywood Shot

- F.T. Ch. Staindrop Murton Marksman
  - Shavington Ted
    - Shavington Ben
      - Shavington Jet
      - Shavington Jess
    - Adderley Thought
      - Adderley Ted
      - F.T. Ch. Adderley Bee
  - Brackenbank Jessie
    - F.T. Ch. Brackenbank Jasper
      - Sudborough Ben
      - Banchory Murton Mystic
    - Brackenbank Belle of Auburn
      - Banchory Jack
      - Quail of Auburn
- Hiwood Peggy. Dam of 4 F.T. Chs.
  - Dual Ch. Staindrop Saighdear
    - Glenhead Jimmy
      - Ch. Kinpurnie Kam
      - Knappies Lass
    - Our Lil
      - F.T. Ch. Glenravil Nimrod
      - Glenravel Glynter
  - Cheverells Sally
    - Cheverells Denny
      - Braeroy Rab
      - F.T. Ch. Cheverells Amber
    - Cheverells Busy Body
      - Balmuto Hewildo
      - F.T. Ch. Cheverells Bustle

FIELD TRIAL CHAMPION GALLEYWOOD SHOT

the alert attentive look of the working Labrador, and in this black dog we have the top winner at Trials for 1957 and 1958. For two years in succession he has won the highest award possible to a working retriever, that of the Kennel Club promoted Retriever Championship. He is extremely well bred, for his sire

Field Trial Champion Staindrop Murton Marksman owned by a great friend of mine, the late Edgar Winter, comes of purely working stock. His grandsire Dual Ch. Staindrop Saighdear was also owned by Edgar Winter, this dog being a yellow, and sire of Shot's dam Hiwood Peggy who is owned by the Hon. Lady Hill-Wood, Peggy being the dam of four Field Trial Champions. Thus you get the very purest of working blood with a touch of the Show Bench through the dual champion, producing a wonderful dog from every point of view. Included in Shot's pedigree you will notice a dog named Glenhead Jimmy, a great north country sire though not himself a Champion. When you consider breeding Labradors you should consider the pedigree of F. T. Ch. Galleywood Shot carefully, for through him and his progeny can be preserved the working instincts of the breed at the highest level.

DUAL CHAMPION KNAITH BANJO

(Owned by Mrs. A. Wormald Glenstuart, Cummertrees, Annan, Dumfries.)

BORN IN 1946, Banjo, who is a Yellow, is both a Field Trial Champion and a Show Champion. Now thirteen years old he is still as active as ever, and is still exhibited—testimony to the longevity and the virility of the Labrador, for Banjo has had an extremely busy life. His owner, Mrs. Wormald, is a great sportswoman, and throughout his life Banjo has been constantly at work at home and at Field Trials all over the country. He has won on the Bench twelve Challenge Certificates and has been Reserve for the honour nine times. He has three Best of Breed awards to his credit. Mrs. Wormald has lost count of the number of firsts he has won which must be well up in the hundreds mark. He has no less than forty-one awards at Field Trials which I should imagine constitutes a record for any gundog.

DUAL CHAMPION KNAITH BANJO

PEDIGREE OF DUAL CHAMPION KNAITH BANJO

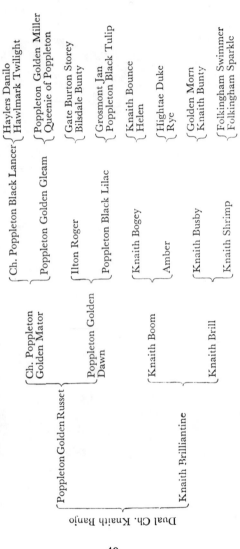

Poppleton Golden Russet
  Ch. Poppleton Golden Mator
    Ch. Poppleton Black Lancer
      Haylers Danilo
      Hawlmark Twilight
    Poppleton Golden Gleam
      Poppleton Golden Miller
      Queenie of Poppleton
  Poppleton Golden Dawn
    Ilton Roger
      Gate Burton Storey
      Bilsdale Bunty
    Poppleton Black Lilac
      Grosmont Jan
      Poppleton Black Tulip

Knaith Brilliantine
  Knaith Boom
    Knaith Bogey
      Knaith Bounce
      Helen
    Amber
      Hightae Duke
      Rye
  Knaith Brill
    Knaith Busby
      Golden Morn
      Knaith Bunty
    Knaith Shrimp
      Folkingham Swimmer
      Folkingham Sparkle

Dual Ch. Knaith Banjo

This widely travelled Labrador lays claim to another interesting record. As constant companion to his mistress, Banjo has shared her room in no less than thirty-three different hotels when travelling to shows of field trials!

FIELD TRIAL CHAMPION
BRACKENBANK JASPER

(Owner Mr. R. N. Burton, Bracken Bank, Lazonby, Cumberland. Bred by Mr. G. Smith.)

IN THE lower illustration on page 43 you see a great dog painted against the background of the moors with a grouse butt included, and just in case you are curious, the recumbent Spaniel you see, I should say is an English Springer, for Mr. Burton has owned many field trial champions in this breed as well as the Labradors.

Born in 1947, Jasper had a wonderful Trial career, running fifteen Open Stakes, two nomination Stakes and only one Novice Stake. He won seven and obtained a place or a mention in all the others. He ran no less than four times in the Retriever Championship winning a second, two thirds, and a Diploma, a truly great and consistent performance over the years.

You may wonder why I have included two pictures of one dog. One is as the artist saw him and the other through the lens of a camera. Thus you will see there has been no 'artistic licence'. Of particular interest is the length of neck in this dog, a necessity in a good retriever when working at speed so that he can gallop with his nose to the ground, without cramping his movement.

Should you intend to become a serious student of breeding, study of Jasper's pedigree linked up with that of F.T. Ch. Galleywood Shot is interesting, for it will be found that Jasper sired the dam of Staindrop Murton Marksman, which in turn sired Galleywood Shot, twice winner of the Retriever Championship.

SPECIAL NOTE. Appearing in Jasper's pedigree and that of Mr. Taylor's Galleywood Shot is the name Glenhead Jimmy. This

PEDIGREE OF FIELD TRIAL CHAMPION BRACKENBANK JASPER

F.T. Ch. Brackenbank Jasper

- Sudborough Ben
  - Greatford Sinner
    - Pettistree Dan
      - Dual Ch. Banchory Painter
      - F.T. Ch. Quest of Wilbury
    - Ketton Venus
      - Hornton Draco
      - Ketton Vice
  - Venus
    - Gateburton Stroller
      - Gateburton Story
      - Gateburton Bounty
    - Jessiebell
      - Vintage
      - Pioneer Judy
- Banchory Murton Mystic
  - Glenhead Jimmy
    - Ch. Kinpurnie Kam
      - Ch. Orchardton Donald
      - F.T. Ch. Kinpurnie Kate
    - Knappies Lass
      - Dual Ch. Bramshaw Bob of Banchory
      - Glenhead Bess
  - Staindrop Hycup Dusk
    - Rust
      - Folkingham Solo
      - Hareshaw Solo
    - Breckonhill Bella
      - F.T. Ch. Font of Flodden
      - F.T. Ch. Tullymurdoch Spanker

FIELD TRIAL CHAMPION BRACKENBANK JASPER

Above, as seen by the camera, and, below an artist's impression.

was a famous North country dog who sire'd a great many winning
and working dogs although he never qualified as Champion himself.

In all breeds and many strains you will find a dog of this
description, a great stud force which through lack of opportunity
or perhaps other reasons never himself acquired the full title.

Mr. Burton owns one of the largest teams of Labradors and
Spaniels in the country and they are regularly worked on his
extensive shootings, where in the season he takes occasional sub-
scribing guns. Exports from his kennel are working for sportsmen all over the world.

FOXHANGER MASCOT C.D.

*(Owned by Lady Elizabeth Simpson, 7 Roedean Crescent, Roehampton,
S.W.15.)*

LADY SIMPSON, wife of Sir Joseph Simpson, Chief Commis-
sioner, Scotland Yard, was indeed fortunate in her first purchase
of a Labrador, as you might well be, for she acquired a black
bitch named Frenchcourt Ripple, which in addition to winning a
Best of Breed award, won the Championship Stake for Tracking
three times, and fifteen field awards in all, including firsts in
Gundog Tests and an Obedience Certificate. Her full title was
Working Trials Champion Frenchcourt Ripple, Track dog
(Excellent) Utility dog (Excellent) and Companion dog (Excellent). She was the foundation of the Foxhanger strain and lived
from 1946 to 1955, and is the Great-Grandmother of Mascot,
subject of our illustration. Although he comes from a straight
line of Black bitches, he himself is a Yellow, his Grandsire being
Dual Ch. Knaith Banjo (see illustration on page 39).

He was bred by Lady Simpson who has trained and won with
him for all types of work and show. His latest wins to start 1959
are First in the puppy and Non-winners Stake at the south
Eastern Gun-dog Society's Working Tests and second in Open
where he beat many older dogs, there being fifteen competitors

PEDIGREE OF FOXHANGER MASCOT C.D.

Foxhanger Mascot C.D.

Copperhill Cheerful
K.C.S.B. 1 Ap.

Foxhanger Lass
K.C.S.B. 1130 AQ (Black)

Copperhill Gillian of Garshangan

Dual Ch. Knaith Banjo

Foxhanger Gay
T.D. ex., U.D. ex., C.D. ex. (Black)

F.T. Ch. Whatstandwell Hiwood Brand

Poppleton Golden Russet
Knaith Brilliantine

Ch. Poppleton Lieutenant
Gigha of Garshangan

Dual Ch. Staindrop Saighdear
Staindrop Carnation (Black)

F.T. Ch. Folkingham Seeker
Working Trial Ch. Frenchcourt
Ripple T.D. ex., U.D. ex.,
C.D. ex. (Black)

45

FOXHANGER MASCOT, C.D.

in each stake. Here again I suggest you link up his breeding with
that of Ch. Banjo.

CHAMPION MIDNIGHT OF MANSERGH

(Owned by Mrs. Roslin Williams, Lilymere, Sedbergh, Yorks.)

THIS DOG completed his Championship under the writer, winning his third Challenge Certificate at Birmingham Ch. Show

PEDIGREE OF CH. MIDNIGHT OF MANSERGH

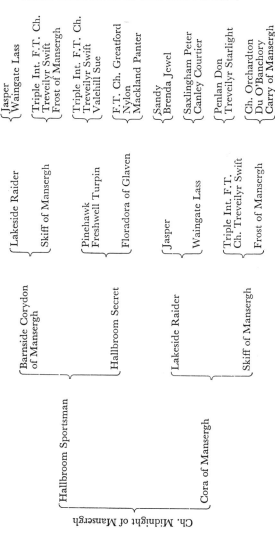

Ch. Midnight of Mansergh

Hallbroom Sportsman

Barnside Corydon of Mansergh

Lakeside Raider
Skiff of Mansergh

Hallbroom Secret

Pinehawk Freshwell Turpin
Floradora of Glaven

Cora of Mansergh

Lakeside Raider

Jasper
Waingate Lass

Skiff of Mansergh

Triple Int. F.T. Ch. Treveilyr Swift
Frost of Mansergh

Jasper
Waingate Lass

Triple Int. F.T. Ch. Treveilyr Swift
Frost of Mansergh

Triple Int. F.T. Ch. Treveilyr Swift
Valehill Sue

F.T. Ch. Greatford Nylon
Mackland Panter

Sandy
Brenda Jewel

Saxlingham Peter
Canley Courtier

Penlan Don
Treveilyr Starlight

Ch. Orchardton Du O'Banchory
Carry of Mansergh

47

CH. MIDNIGHT OF MANSERGH

where he was also judged best gundog all breeds. He is sire of both a Challenge Certificate winner (Bumblekite of Mansergh) and an Open Stake winner at field trials (Brysia Ben). His daughter Bumblekite, still under two years of age, has won two awards for best exhibit in show all breeds, and a Reserve Challenge Certificate as well as one Certificate. Midnight has sired many Championship Show winners and at least four winners of awards at Field Trials, as well as four Best in Show winners. A great record in a highly competitive breed.

CHAMPION RULER OF BLAIRCOURT

(Owned by Mr. and Mrs. Grant Cairns, 50, First Gardens, Dumbreck, Glasgow, S.1.)

FOREVER FAMOUS Ruler will go down in history as the Labrador to distinguish himself at Crufts 1959 in winning the Certificate and best of breed, went on to the Best Gundog and finally was runner-up for the supreme award of Best in Show, a truly great performance by a young dog. In 1958 I had the pleasure of awarding him the Challenge Certificate at the Labrador Retriever Club's own show. In all he has won Ten Challenge Certificates, twice reserve for the honour, and has been best of breed on six occasions.

The pedigree of Ruler is of considerable interest to serious breeders for you will find Craigluscar Dusk of Blaircourt as Grandmother on both sides of his pedigree. This is a means used by breeders to establish in a strain the virtues of a good female line. Incidentally through this breeding the dog named Glenhead Jimmie again appears. In some pedigrees the name is spelt Jimmy—still the same dog. You will find particular reference to this dog in the pedigree of Mr. Burton's Champion on page 42.

Through Ruler you will appreciate that Jimmie was equally good a sire of show dogs as workers, or may I put it in a better way he was a sire of workers which were also good lookers.

The high honours won by Mr. and Mrs. Grant Cairns of Glasgow should be an encouragement to all young breeders.

CH. RULER OF BLAIRCOURT

PEDIGREE OF CHAMPION RULER OF BLAIRCOURT

Ch. Ruler of Blaircourt	Forbes of Blaircourt	Treesholme Thunder	Triumph of Treesholme
			{ Lochar Gold Flake { Poppleton Golden Sherry
			Treesholme Tune
			{ Int. Ch. Donnybrook Thunder { Treesholme Twilight
		Craigluscar Dusk of Blaircourt	Darkie of Elmbank
			{ Glenhead Jimmie { Sheba of Crombie
			Craigluscar Black Gem
			{ Black Eagle of Glengour { Black Arrogance of Glengour
	Olivia of Blaircourt	Lawrie of Blaircourt	Treesholme Trigger
			{ Int. Ch. Donnybrook Thunder { Treesholme Twilight
			Fiona of Blaircourt
			{ Treesholme Thunder { Craigluscar Dusk of Blaircourt
		Craigluscar Dusk of Blaircourt	Darkie of Elmbank
			{ Glenhead Jimmie { Sheba of Crombie
			Craigluscar Black Gem
			{ Black Eagle of Glengour { Black Arrogance of Glengour

CHAMPION HOLTON BARON

(Owner Mr. M. C. W. Gilliat, The Bough, Burwash Common, Sussex.)

IN THIS famous black dog we probably have the biggest winner of the post-war era, for Baron has won twenty-five Challenge Certificates and been best of breed nineteen times and has won in addition thirteen Reserve Certificates. He has been in two successive years best Black Labrador at Crufts. In all in top class shows he has won eighty-nine firsts and thirty-five seconds. He is also a great worker and has won four Certificates of Merit at Field Trials including one in the Labrador Club's Open Stake, where he also won the Challenge Cup for the best looking dog or bitch at the meeting. For four successive years Baron was best of breed at the Ladies Kennel Association Ch. Show and he held a similar honour for three consecutive years at the Brighton Ch. Show, where one year he was reserve best exhibit in show all breeds. He has won at Open Shows Best exhibit under Mrs. Pacey, our great international all-round judge, who, in addition to awarding him Challenge Certificates, made him best exhibit in a big entry at the Hertfordshire Show where I said of him 'There are many dogs of various breeds I admire, but Baron is a dog I like as well as admire', indicative of the great character of the dog.

Mr. Gilliat is a very old breeder, his kennel being established long before the war, and his Holton prefix has been in evidence in the top awards at shows throughout the years.

CHAMPION DIANT JULIET

(Owner—Mrs. L. Wilson Jones, Norton, Bury St. Edmunds.)

THIS YELLOW bitch is pure yellow bred for generations. The lovely untouched out of doors and unposed picture of her conveys her all round excellence. She was top bitch either colour in 1958 and has won fifteen challenge certificates, including Best of Breed at Crufts, and I had the pleasure of naming her Best exhibit either sex at the Labrador Club's own championship show.

CHAMPION HOLTON BARON

PEDIGREE OF CHAMPION HOLTON BARON

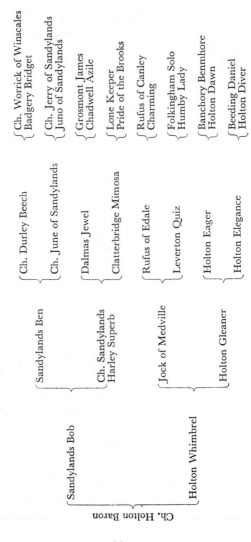

Ch. Holton Baron

Sandylands Bob

  Sandylands Ben
    Ch. Durley Beech
      Ch. Worrick of Winscales
      Badgery Bridget
    Ch. June of Sandylands
      Ch. Jerry of Sandylands
      Juno of Sandylands

  Ch. Sandylands Harley Superb
    Dalmas Jewel
      Grosmont James
      Chadwell Azile
    Clatterbridge Mimosa
      Lone Keeper
      Pride of the Brooks

Holton Whimbrel

  Jock of Medville
    Rufus of Edale
      Rufus of Canley
      Charming
    Leverton Quiz
      Folkingham Solo
      Humby Lady

  Holton Gleaner
    Holton Eager
      Banchory Benmhore
      Holton Dawn
    Holton Elegance
      Beeding Daniel
      Holton Diver

Photo: C. M. Cooke

CHAMPION DIANT JULIET

PEDIGREE OF CHAMPION DIANT JULIET

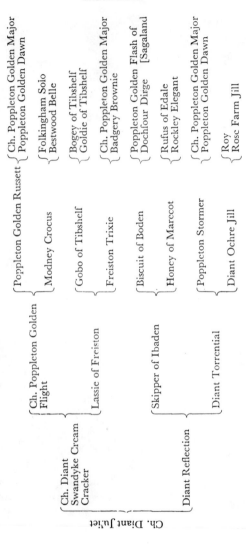

Ch. Diant Juliet

Ch. Diant Swandyke Cream Cracker
— Ch. Poppleton Golden Flight
—— Poppleton Golden Russett
——— Ch. Poppleton Golden Major
——— Poppleton Golden Dawn
—— Modney Crocus
——— Folkingham Solo
——— Bestwood Belle
— Lassie of Freiston
—— Gobo of Tibshelf
——— Bogey of Tibshelf
——— Goldie of Tibshelf
—— Freiston Trixie
——— Ch. Poppleton Golden Major
——— Badgery Brownie

Diant Reflection
— Skipper of Ibaden
—— Biscuit of Boden
——— Poppleton Golden Flash of [Sagaland
——— Dochlour Dirge
—— Honey of Marccot
——— Rufus of Edale
——— Rockley Elegant
— Diant Torrential
—— Poppleton Stormer
——— Ch. Poppleton Golden Major
——— Poppleton Golden Dawn
—— Diant Ochre Jill
——— Roy
——— Rose Farm Jill

56

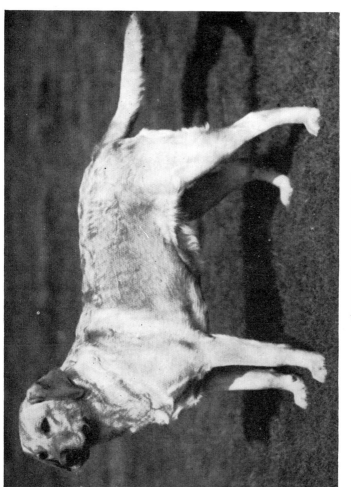

CHAMPION KINLEY MELODY

PEDIGREE OF CHAMPION KINLEY MELODY

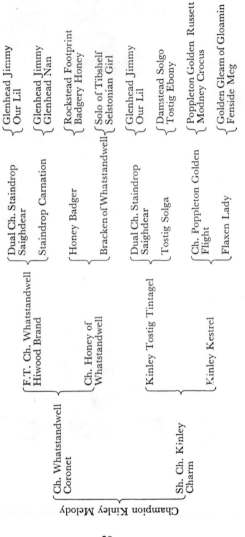

Champion Kinley Melody

- Ch. Whatstandwell Coronet
  - F.T. Ch. Whatstandwell Hiwood Brand
    - Dual Ch. Staindrop Saighdear
      - Glenhead Jimmy
      - Our Lil
    - Staindrop Carnation
      - Glenhead Jimmy
      - Glenhead Nan
  - Ch. Honey of Whatstandwell
    - Honey Badger
      - Rockstead Footprint
      - Badgery Honey
    - Bracken of Whatstandwell
      - Solo of Tibshelf
      - Selstonian Girl
- Sh. Ch. Kinley Charm
  - Kinley Tostig Tintagel
    - Dual Ch. Staindrop Saighdear
      - Glenhead Jimmy
      - Our Lil
    - Tostig Solga
      - Damstead Solgo
      - Tostig Ebony
  - Kinley Kestrel
    - Ch. Poppleton Golden Flight
      - Poppleton Golden Russett
      - Modney Crocus
    - Flaxen Lady
      - Golden Gleam of Gloamin
      - Fenside Meg

58

She started 1959 well by winning Certificate and Best of Breed at the big Manchester Show. She has many notable variety wins to her credit including the Sporting Group at Chester Ch. Show and Best Gundog Bitch at the Bath Ch. Show.

CHAMPION KINLEY MELODY

(Owned by Mr. Fred G. Wrigley, Greenhills, Dalton Magna, Rotherham.)

THIS YELLOW bitch is one of the best in the breed either colour on the bench at the present time. During 1958 she won four challenge certificates, twice best of breed, and six Reserve Certificates. Her owner is a great sportsman who plays a leading part in Labrador Club affairs. As one would expect Melody is a fine worker as well as show dog.

CHAPTER 4

BUYING AND TRAINING A LABRADOR PUPPY

THE purchase of this book suggests that you are already committed in your choice of dog, and you can be assured you will not make a better one out of all the gun dog breeds.

Presuming you have not actually bought a Labrador, I think the simplest way of acquiring one is to purchase a well-bred puppy. Now there are hundreds of good breeders of Labradors in this country; I suggest you go to one of them, tell them exactly the circumstances in which you live, explain to them the exact purpose for which you require the dog, or the bitch, and put yourself unreservedly in their hands. You might think the big breeders are too expensive; actually they are not. The fact that you buy from a well-known breeder and kennel is an insurance that you will get every satisfaction in whatever class of stock you may buy. These people are very proud of their dogs and their reputations, and they will take an interest in anything they may sell you, and will always be available to give helpful advice on your youngster, should some problems arise in rearing.

If, however, you follow out the simple precautions, the simple instructions I hope to give you later in this book, there is no need to have any qualms about buying a young dog, for with the advent of antidistemper and hard pad serum your troubles compared with those of owners years ago are negligible. I would advise you, even though you should have to pay a couple of guineas more for your puppy, to ask the breeder to have the puppy Epivaxed—this is an insurance against the maladies I have mentioned—and the veterinary surgeon who gives the injections will also sign a document to the effect that this has been done.

I quite appreciate that you would like to know something on how to choose a puppy, even though you are going to place yourselves in the hands of a good breeder. In the first place, look for a puppy that is well developed, sleek in its coat, with a kind, gentle eye, small ears, level mouth, nice broad foreface, sturdy limbs, finished with good pads, a short body with great ribs, and particularly, look out for one with a short tail. A great feature in the Labrador Retriever is the otter-shaped tail, thick at the root, short and tapering to a blunt end. Another great feature, of course, in the Labrador is the water-resisting coat, soft under-coat, and harsher outer coat, but only experience—and a lot of experience at that—will enable you to judge how a puppy's coat will finish. On this you have got to rely on the breeding of your puppy; you may, of course, be able to see the bitch, and thus judge to some extent how your puppy should turn out.

I am very often asked which I would recommend a beginner to own, a dog puppy or a bitch puppy. There are certain seasonal drawbacks of course to a bitch, and if you're a shooting man and only need one animal, I would suggest a dog, the reason being that he will not break down in the middle of the shooting season as happens sometimes in a bitch. To those who just need a com-panion, I suggest they choose a bitch; they have a softer nature, are very home loving, and are not inclined to wander the streets, as will a dog at times, answering in his healthy youth the urges of nature and sex, very often to the discomfiture of his owner.

It has been suggested to me that bitches may accidentally become mated. In the first place there are many modern prepara-tions on the market which will repel a dog from a bitch in this condition, but should your bitch get mated and you are aware of the fact, get into a car or taxi and go straight to the veterinary surgeon telling him exactly what has happened. He may, with his specialized knowledge, very often prevent conception taking place through a mongrel or stray dog.

Still on the subject, it has been proved a fallacy that if a pure bred bitch has been mated to a mongrel dog, she is ruined as a breeding proposition. This was firmly believed for many, many years by many, many people, but it is entirely erroneous. If your bitch is mated by a street dog and has her litter, you can dispose of them as your conscience or opportunity presents, and at her next season, you can with confidence mate her to a pure bred dog, and you will get pure bred puppies.

Should your bitch get astray, and become mated to another thoroughbred dog, say for instance, a Border Collie, or perhaps a Retriever of another breed, it will be found, if you have the opportunity to rear these puppies, that they are really first-class companions and highly intelligent dogs. They are not mongrels; they are the first cross between two pure breeds, and in this connection I have found that a cross between a Labrador and a Border Collie—the type of collie you see working for the shepherds on the hills and the moors, when reaching the adult stage —becomes one of the finest pupils possible for the guide dog for the blind training centres. They are biddable and intelligent and actually seem to present the combination of the better qualities in both individual breeds. In a chance mating, I should say put the puppies down, but should you know that your bitch has been mated to a thoroughbred then there is a distinct outlet for the puppies without the harrowing experience of having to destroy them.

Let us imagine you are already the proud owner of a well-bred, well-grown, Epivaxed puppy of two to three months old. Naturally you want to know how to rear and train him. Chapters on puppy rearing and puppy training are naturally complementary each to the other but first I will deal purely with training the puppy, and the following chapter deals with the question of puppy rearing. It is a wise old saying that the way to a puppy's heart is by way of his stomach and in the feeding of your dog you can start his earliest training. In the first place, feed at regular hours. This in itself is the first step to your dog becoming a well-behaved animal and regular in his habits. Just owning the one puppy you are more fortunate than the kennel owner who cannot always give the same attention to a litter as you will be able to do with your individual. For instance, when you have prepared your puppy food you can place it on the floor in sight of the puppy, meanwhile restraining him with your other hand. Though he may struggle hard, restrain him for a short period and then allow him to take his food. After a time he will soon realize that he cannot just dash across and eat whenever he thinks fit and here you have got the first step towards obedience.

Make him sit down now. Press his backside gently to the floor using the word 'sit'. He will soon get to know this very simple word of three letters which is one of the most important words in the vocabulary of a trained Labrador. People will tell you stories of the almost uncanny intelligence of dogs and some will over-emphasize their reasoning powers, but I can assure you the cleverest puppy or a dog is nowhere comparable to a little child of two, therefore you must be the more patient in the exercises you wish the dog to perform on his way to complete obedience.

During the simple exercise I have described to you, you can also lay the foundation to that most desirable thing in a dog, complete cleanliness in the house. Immediately the puppy has finished his food and had a drink, he should be put outside for it is a matter of course that a full stomach will encourage him in the natural acts. In quite a short time you will find your dog will associate food with this second little exercise, and rather than being put out he will naturally go to the door and wait for you to open it for him. It will come as a surprise to find how soon this gets to be a matter of complete routine, and what a great thing this will be when later in life the dog has more control over himself, that, when left alone, instead of soiling the house, he will wait for your return. But in this regard I do urge upon you not to leave the dog too long alone in the house. It is cruel when you have trained a dog to be house clean you should put too great a strain upon him in resisting the very calls of nature.

It is one of the most natural things in the world for a young puppy to jump up—by that he rears up on his back legs and paws at your trousers or skirt. While a puppy this isn't so objectionable and, in playing with him, some people might even encourage him to do this, but you are laying the seeds of trouble for the future if you allow it. There is nothing more annoying to a lady, or a man for that matter, than a dog with muddy feet to jump up and draw its feet down a very smart skirt or a pair of trousers. Therefore, encourage your puppy to keep all four feet on the ground and you can teach him to do this by repressing him with your hand, at the same time using the word 'down'. This exercise of repression with the word 'down' will soon have results and you can, at the same time, encourage the rest of your family to take the same action, and for that matter, visitors as well. The dog will soon get to know that he is not allowed to jump up, and he will be a happier dog for this little exercise, since he will very likely escape in the future many a cuffed ear for fouling skirts or trousers or laddering a pair of valuable nylon stockings.

Before continuing with my very simple hints on pup rearing, I must point out by this time your puppy should be christened and whenever you are teaching him these simple little acts, always associate the name of the dog with the name of the exercise, such as 'Sit, Mac', 'Down, Mac' and when you start your lessons in more general obedience, keep up the name with the action until as time goes on you will be able to drop this.

Now is the time to indulge in one very important exercise. It is the complaint of many dog owners that when they call their dog it simply will not come to them and there is nothing in this world more aggravating than a disobedient dog; in fact, a disobedient dog can be a dangerous dog, particularly if he should be loose on the road amongst traffic. A disobedient adult dog is generally the result of slackness during puppy training and therefore I cannot emphasize too much the importance of this simple exercise which we might term 'the recall'.

A puppy, whatever time of the day you may choose to indulge in this exercise, will always respond to a tit-bit; therefore have some little thing that he appreciates in your hand when you start this exercise. By this time he will know his name and when the puppy is running about just sharply shout his name, 'Mac'. This will create his attention and then you can use one of several terms. You might say 'Come here' or just simply 'Here', or you may say 'Come in' or 'Come to me'. Choose the one which suits you and discard all the others. If eventually you intend using your dog for shooting, I would recommend the term 'Come in', but more of this later. Otherwise, just the simple term 'Here, Mac' with encouraging movements of the hands will probably result in the puppy running towards you. When he arrives pat him and give him his little tit-bit and then let him away again.

You can indulge in this simple little exercise two or three times and no more, but make sure that you always finish on good terms with your puppy. The last exercise should always be well done. You give the call 'Here, Mac' or 'Come in Mac' and, on the puppy running straight to you, pat him, reward him and your little lesson always finishes with a pleasant feeling between the two of you. Never by any chance give up in despair at his disobedience, and on the other hand do not bore the puppy by too often repeating the exercise.

While on the subject of this choice of commands, the first word I told you to use for your puppy was 'Sit', but if your dog is eventually to be a shooting dog I should just suggest you couple up with this the word 'Up' or 'Hup'. This is the general term used in the shooting field to make your dog sit down. It's a short, sharp term that you can use when the dog is quite a long way from you and it is one that is in general use amongst the best trainers. You can still use the word 'Sit' and this is used when the dog is by your side. Eventually your dog will sit down just to a hiss between the teeth. The best trainers are all the most quiet in making their commands.

Assuming that you do not require your dog to go shooting, I personally rather like the words 'Come to me' as a command for recall. This might be just my own personal preference but it is one I gained through a long association with the finest dog trainers in the world and these are the moorland shepherds. When they have their sheep brought to them by these marvellous sheep dogs, in close work if they want the dog to approach to them, still keeping a wary eye on the sheep, they use the term 'Come to me'.

Labrador Retriever puppies will naturally pick up and carry anything around in their mouths and there is nothing they like to do better than to chase a ball. Another useful early exercise is to train your dog with a ball. The idea in this exercise is to turn the dog's natural carrying instinct to doing this natural inclination at your command. I shouldn't attempt this exercise unless you are quite confident that the dog knows your commands of 'Sit' and 'Up', and that he will obey them. To make quite sure, I suggest you put a light lead round your puppy's neck and tell him to sit. Then throw the ball a short distance away and the puppy will naturally try to gallop after it. But force him down into the sit position, repeating the word 'Sit' and you can also use the word 'No'.

This is a word you will find of great value right throughout the dog's life in controlling him. The earlier he gets to know this simple little word the easier it will be for your future training of the dog. He will soon realize that 'No' is a repressive term and you do not want him to continue what he is doing. You have thrown your ball; the puppy being at the sit he tries to chase, you restrain him with your light check cord round his neck; you put him down to the sit position and you say 'No' when he wants to go, put him down and say 'Sit'. When you have got him steady, leave him sitting for just a few seconds, then free him with the word 'Fetch it'. Off the puppy will go and pick up the ball and as soon as he has done this use your command of 'Here, Mac', 'Come here Mac' or 'Come to me Mac'. The puppy may be inclined to run about and play on the return, but still encourage him and when he comes to you, gently remove the ball from his mouth and pat him, make a fuss of him, 'Good dog, good dog' and give him the tit-bits he likes. By repeating this exercise with its suitable reward, in addition to the dog enjoying what to him at the moment is a game, he begins to know that he is pleasing you and that he gathers a reward for doing so. Later on you'll be able to dispense with the reward for he will realize as he gets older that he and you are a partnership—you look after him and he tries to please you.

In starting him off from your side to collect the ball, you could use the words 'Fetch it' or 'Seek it', particularly if the ball has gone out of sight. In fact, after you have indulged in this exercise for some time and the puppy responds readily to it, sits steadily, goes out when you say 'Fetch it', brings the ball back, sits down again on command and gives you the ball and then takes his reward, you can purposely throw the ball somewhere where it finishes out of sight. Then you can use the words 'Seek it', and the puppy will soon associate the words 'Seek it' with the assumption that the object he has to fetch back to you cannot be seen with his eyes. This is a very very important exercise, for, especially if he is to be a shooting dog, it is obvious anyone can pick up the game which can be seen. His chief value is to find the game which isn't seen. Thus if, for instance, a pheasant is lying out in the open, is too far for you to pick it up yourself, you send your dog and you say 'Fetch it', but if the pheasant has fallen into cover and perhaps the dog has not seen exactly where the bird has fallen, you tell the dog to seek it, or, a term which is generally used in the field trial world, is 'High lost'.

Now this seems to be rather extending the number of words of command very rapidly for a dog so young. I suggest you take your choice and restrict your commands to the minimum and in the most simple form. Reiteration will soon impress the command on the dog's memory and reward will soon associate him with work well done. You have already taught him the word 'No', and any time when indulging in these slightly more advanced exercises the dog goes off at a tangent, does something wrong, you just repress him with the simple word 'No', and then repeat the command you had just previously given to him.

By this time your dog should be getting a very good idea of what is required of him and becoming quite an obedient puppy. He will sit down, he will come to you when he is called, he'll go away when you send him and, persevering, you will find that he responds quickly and smartly to the words of command he knows. Then comes the time to do these exercises while on the move. As a first step you must train your puppy to walk on a lead. This requires a little patience but an intelligent, well-bred puppy soon becomes used to the restriction of the lead and if he persists in pulling ahead, just take a folded up newspaper, tap him over the nose and, pulling the lead towards you, say 'Back' or 'Heel', or 'Heel up' or 'Come to heel'. Take your choice of these terms and just use one of them. He will soon know that it pays him to walk quietly by your side and if you are starting off a dog to be used in the shooting field, make it the left side —unless you are left-handed yourself—because if you are right-handed and carrying a gun in your right hand, it is advisable to have the dog walking on your left.

When you have got the dog quite used to walking steadily at your side on the lead you can dispense with the lead altogether and continue this exercise until you have reasonable confidence that your puppy will stay with you and walk nicely to heel. This will take some considerable time for it is very natural in the young to want to dash around and play, but by gently repressing him and extending the exercise for a little longer each day you will soon get results. Immediately you find you have complete control of the puppy then you can indulge in the exercise you taught in the home or in your garden; that is, throw the ball away, drop the puppy to the word 'Sit', send him for it and reward him and then say 'Heel' and then walk along together.

When you have successfully accomplished this and repeated it over a period, then you can try another simple exercise. Send your dog away from you and then use the sharp word 'Hup' and make him sit down when he is away from your side. This is a very good exercise for the day may come that your dog is running about and exercising himself, say when you are crossing a field which unknowingly may contain some cattle. The first thing is to stop him, and if he has been well-trained to the word 'Hup' you shout 'Hup' and down he sits. Then 'Come to me' and he returns and then keep him to heel. This is the very successful outcome of exercises well carried out in the first place, and you will be surprised by the time the dog is six months old how well you are on the way to having that greatest of all possessions, a completely happy but well-trained young puppy.

Training a puppy to become a gun dog is quite an art in itself and whole books have been written on this subject. I have barely touched on it here, but it is advisable even when teaching your puppy general obedience, to have in mind what you want the dog for eventually. Even so the terms and exercises outlined above will be of value were the dog to go into full training as a gun dog later in his life. They are, of course, of untold value in ensuring his general good behaviour as a companion dog.

Properly carried out, these very simple exercises should result in your being able to trust your dog in most circumstances, but I really want you to take my advice; however well trained your dog may be, if you are on the road where there is any traffic whatsoever, keep your dog on a lead. You might say—and I have been guilty myself in saying—'My dog will not do anything wrong. My dog is under perfect control.' He may be, but some unruly dog might rush at your dog who, in turn, might jump away off the footpath straight under the wheel of a passing car or cause a car to swerve, causing an accident which might involve injury to other people. Therefore do have your dog on the lead all the time on the main roads or on the subsidiary roads.

When you are going across country, of course, you can give the dog his liberty, let him have a gallop on common land or fields where there are no cattle to disturb. Again, when you come into villages, if you are in doubt be on the safe side; put him on the lead; do not be ashamed of doing so; it is not a sign of weakness on your part.

It is a great satisfaction to take a well-trained puppy or young dog into public and see him behave well and note how other people appreciate the results of your training, but you should remember that not all people are dog lovers. Your dog has led a happy life, he has not been too restricted in his training, and he is full of confidence where other people are concerned. But I do suggest you restrain him approaching other people. I know many are guilty of encouraging a dog away from its owner; you can't avoid this, but on the other hand you can restrain your dog, without giving offence to other dog lovers who are unwittingly trying to ruin your good training by calling the dog to them without your permission. Endeavour to keep the dog under good control at all times and in all circumstances.

Let us just go through the doggy vocabulary again. We start with the word 'Sit' and the word 'Up'; then we progress to the words 'Come to me' or 'Come here'; then 'Seek it', 'High lost', 'Seek lost', 'Find it'; the words 'Heel' and 'Heel up' and, of course, I may have overlooked two very important words of command and that is 'Lie down'. A dog that is used to the 'Sit' command will soon respond to the command 'Lie down' for he is partly towards fulfilling this command having been taught the word 'Sit'.

In the general training of your puppy, who I presume is to live in the house, from the very first I strongly suggest that you appropriate some corner, warm and free from draughts, and place a box or basket there with a rug in it, and teach the dog to know that it is his home. Encourage him to go there when he is tired. Say 'To bed', 'On your bed' and he will soon know what you mean. It is very nice to have your favourite dog during the evening enjoying the warmth of the fire from which you can both take mutual pleasure; but before you retire for the night give him the word of command 'On your bed' and see that he goes there and what is more, stays there. Puppies are imitative; they see you lying on a couch, they see you sitting on a chair, and they naturally want to do the same thing. Here you must be firm and stop them from the very first time they attempt to use either the chairs or settees in your home. 'Down' is the word to use, or 'No' if he attempts it again, and, if he persists, a rolled-up newspaper and a smart crack over the nose will soon convince him that it is better to stay where you want him than to try and join you on something forbidden to him.

These are very simple exercises I have suggested, but they are absolutely essential if you are going later to enjoy many, many years of happy companionship from a well-trained and happy dog. I do strongly suggest that you make every endeavour to carry them out one by one and persevere until each exercise is accomplished in a perfectly satisfactory manner. And remember, reward your dog every time he does something to please you. Later, of course, you can dispense with the rewards because he comes to know exactly what you want him to do, and the pleasure in your voice expressed in the words 'Good dog' and the occasional pat are reward enough. If you are cross with him he will soon know the inflection in your voice and will take notice. I have found an intelligent, well-trained dog can be more upset or repressed by sternness in a voice than a blow. In fact, I hope if you carry out what I have suggested, that you have no recourse to sternness in your commands, nor to chastisement of your dog.

If you should wish to extend the training of your dog and, particularly, if you want to train him as a gun dog, I cannot do better than recommend to you a book written a long time ago by a great personal friend of mine, Mr. Dick Sharpe. He was a great sportsman and a wonderful gun dog trainer. He ran dogs at field trials and judged them and for many years he was Kennel Editor of the *Shooting Times*. This book by him is called *Dog Training by Amateurs* and is described as a handbook of instruction for all sportsmen. Dick Sharpe's methods of training were so sound and effective in practice that one year before the war at Crufts

International Dog Show, when it was held in the Agricultural Hall at Islington, he undertook to train a gun dog puppy in the ring in the midst of all that great assembly of dogs and people. There was no fake about this; anyone could submit their young dog for training by his method. There were thousands of people round that ringside that evening, I remember, and Dick Sharpe made a wonderful job in under an hour in taking a raw puppy and teaching him quite reasonable obedience in that short time. The demonstration of his methods did much to convince people that they were the best methods to follow and I personally benefited largely from reading this book that I recommend to you now.

May I quote just one paragraph from the foreword to this book, which bears out to a great extent what I have tried to tell you in the treatment of your young puppy.

The extract is this:

'The fundamental rule always cropping up is the prevention of error, and guidance into the path of strict rectitude. "Train a child in the way it should go" is an injunction as sound for animals as for human beings. Its application is not always obvious, for between the sin and withholding the opportunity to commit it is a missing link, which mere intelligence on the part of the would-be trainer can hardly be expected to forge. But with an instructor who has gauged the limits of canine intelligence, who has based rules on long observation of many dispositions and has found out how to convey wishes that can never be explained by word of mouth, the veriest novice, provided he or she possesses the qualification of sympathy, can progress by slow and steady stages towards obedience and understanding.'

Treat the puppy as you would treat a child and, to my mind, it is a marvellous thing if a little child be given a puppy of its own. Mind you, you have to train them both but with the child and the puppy growing up together they seem to both develop in their own small and fascinating ways, and a live toy, a live puppy, is much better than the finest mechanical toy that was ever made.

CHAPTER 5

PUPPY REARING

WHEN buying a single puppy, you will probably not acquire it before eight to ten weeks of age, and then the owner will be very pleased to tell you how the puppy has been weaned, and what it is being fed at the time you take it over. You should continue on these lines for the time being.

As early as you can I always advise giving a little raw meat. You can afford some good, lean, butcher's meat, and scrape it. Don't cut it into lumps, scrape it and add a little to the normal puppy meal, for the evening feed. After all, raw meat is the natural food of the dog.

When I was actively engaged in puppy rearing, I always contracted with my butcher to take all his brisket bones. Now a brisket bone is mostly gristle, and you can give the puppies as many of these as you like. No harm will be done, and they can chew and chew and chew on them; they'll act as their own dentists, their milk teeth will disappear, and you will find their second teeth will come strong and healthy and clean.

There are all sorts of aids to puppy rearing, with all sorts of claims made for them, but apart from feeding a good puppy food, reinforced with any of the patent milks, plus some lean meat, the only help I gave my puppies was a mixture of 50 per cent cod liver oil and Colloidal Parrish's chemical food. I suggest the Colloidal form, for this is the only way in which a puppy can fully assimilate the food. A teaspoonful a day of this mixture, increased to a dessertspoonful at six months, ensures them producing good bone and they have no trouble with their teeth. It also aids pigmentation and is a good general tonic.

The simple fare that I have outlined, with a helping of the suggested mixture is the way I reared my many champions: simple, good food, while they are puppies, and little and often. As they gradually grow older, drop down the meals until the adult dogs will live happily on, say, one hard dog biscuit or one meat bone in the morning, and a good feed of hound meal reinforced with meat, vegetables and general scraps in the evening. The dog flourishes on variety like we do, but always remember his basic diet, try and give him a supply of good fresh meat and good bones for him to chew.

Above all, don't overfeed your Labrador—this, however, doesn't mean putting him on a starvation diet. The following amusing story appeared in a daily newspaper recently, under the heading of 'ADVICE', and helps to illustrate very well the point I am trying to make.

'Walking in Mayfair the other day, I saw a local resident feeding his Labrador dog on the pavement outside his home. The dog was large and so was his dinner.

'The dog-owner was rather startled when a large man tapped him with a walking-stick and told him in no uncertain way that the dog was too fat and he was feeding it far too much.

'The owner listened carefully and appeared grateful for the advice. But one thing he did not know—his unsolicited instructor was the Earl of Rosebery!'

Puppies up to three months old, invariably carry worms of a certain type. Don't let this trouble you unduly, for today there are excellent vermifuges available to everyone. Their administration is detailed and carefully explained, and using any one of these you will find it quite simple to free your dog from these parasites.

Later in life, a dog can be infected with a different type of worm altogether—the tape worm. A gun dog is particularly susceptible to tape worms for, running the fields, especially where there have been sheep about, and using his nose, he can inhale the spores, which eventually become that most common affliction in a gun dog. The obvious sign of infestation to be seen is in the dog's droppings, otherwise you may notice his general lack of condition, staring coat and a little scalding of the hair below the eyes. With these symptoms you can be fairly sure that your dog is infected. Any chemist will advise you, or give you the choice of several very fine treatments that have been patented, although when I was in the kennels with my manager we always used a 10 minim capsule for an adult dog after keeping him without food for up to twenty-four hours. After one capsule and then a reasonable amount of castor oil, the dog is given his liberty in a field or some open space. This method was very often effective and the dog would be freed from tape worms for quite a long time to come.

People often ask me how much exercise a puppy should have during the day. Well, I have always found that if you have two or three puppies together, they will exercise themselves. Where there is only one, I suggest you can yourself, or your children, play with it with a ball, but only do it until the pup is reasonably exercised, and not over-tired.

As soon as a puppy is properly weaned and is thriving well, you can teach him to follow you around on a lead. You must have patience, but don't forget that the best approach to a puppy is through his stomach, so a little bit of his favourite food in your hand will encourage him not to try and bolt when you put the lead round his neck. Controlled exercise as the dog gets older is the finest of all. I advocate good brisk road walking to everyone wishing to produce a good strong young dog, particularly if you want to have him good on his pads, well muscled and fit, for the showing that you might visualize in the future. There is no reason why, when you have bought a first class puppy, eventually you should not show him, but if this is your intention I do suggest you take greatest care of his feeding, and also of his exercise. I advocate also regular grooming, a harsh, stiff brush or a good stout hand-glove, and a brisk rub over twice a day if you like. You'll put a polish on his coat and the massage will do him good, physically and generally.

Actually, the whole question of rearing a puppy is a matter of common sense; I keep reiterating that a puppy should be treated almost like a child. Kindness and a little discipline, regular meals and the personal attention and affection of an owner will bring wonderful results. You'll get endless interest and considerable amusement in guiding the steps of your puppy in the way they should go. Always, when training the puppy, keep in mind what you ultimately require, be it a guard dog, just a companion dog or a shooting dog. Thus, you may vary intelligently some of the words of command and perhaps part of the treatment in rearing, but in the main the advice I have given applies to practically any gun dog puppy whatever its ultimate use may be.

CHAPTER 6

BREEDING

SHOULD you like to save time and are very keen to breed a Labrador for yourself, I would suggest you go to a good kennel and ask them to sell you a proved brood bitch from which they have had possibly one or two litters. You have the advantage of being able to find out what the bitch has produced, and, as they have plenty of her stock or as much of her stock as they require, they would very possibly sell her to you at a reasonable figure, particularly to a good home and where the rest of her life could be happily lived in retirement after she had given you the litter you seek.

Alternatively, you might go to a kennel and ask them if they would loan you a bitch on what we call breeding terms. There is a special agreement provided for this type of transaction and I strongly recommend that one of these agreements should be properly filled out and filed with the Kennel Club. However reliable both parties may be, it is always advisable in all these cases to have everything set out in detail and in writing. You make your own terms: it may be suggested that you take the bitch, and the owner of the bitch shall name which dog to which she must be mated. You will then take her to the dog, pay the stud fee, and then probably you would choose alternately a puppy from the resultant litter, the owner taking first, third, fifth, you take second, fourth and sixth. When the puppies are of the age to leave their mother, back she goes with the puppies the owner is to keep, and you are left with three puppies of a very good breeding to which you can attach your name and, if you wish, your own particular prefix. A prefix consists of a kennel name that is registered with the Kennel Club and which no one else can use. You may pay a yearly fee for this, or a lump sum, and you can claim this title in perpetuity. As I have mentioned already, Lady Howe's famous prefix is that of Banchory; my own is that of Beauchief.

After the litter is born it will help the bitch to augment her ration with plenty of good fresh milk. Later, when the puppies will start to lap a little milk, at perhaps three weeks of age, buy a first grade milk food, and feed them according to directions. There is nothing to beat the bitch's milk, but this will help her particularly when there is a big litter and the bitch is not over-supplied with her own natural milk. There are a number of good milk foods on the market, all very reliable, all manners of feeding clearly defined, and the whole thing has been made extremely simple.

If you follow one of my suggestions and take a bitch on breeding terms, the owner nominates the sire, of course, and this frees you from a most important problem and that is finding a suitable mate for your bitch. Let us, however, take the case of just the individual bitch you have reared from a puppy. I suggest you should miss her the first time she is ready for breeding and wait until the second time, which will probably be twelve to fourteen months old. By this time, and assuming that you have joined one of the breed clubs, you will have gained a little insight into Labradors generally and you may be able to choose one from the numerous stud dogs advertised, otherwise I would suggest you ask one of the Club officials for their advice. Always take along the pedigree because on this, above all, depends the choice of a stud dog. You must choose one whose pedigree is suitable for that of your bitch.

There are three different classes of champion now in gun dogs; one is a field trial champion, which has won high honours in the shooting field competitions; second is a show champion, which has won some high honours just for beauty; and thirdly there is another title just the simple one of champion. This means that the dog has won high honours on the show bench and has also been taken to a field trial and proved that it will work and shows all the hereditary instincts of the breed. Either the first or the third are the ones I suggest you choose as a mate for your Labrador. If you are not particularly interested in the exhibition side, choose a working dog of great intelligence, but if you fancy perhaps you would like to breed some show dogs, then sort out a dog with the simple title champion, not show champion. It does ensure that you will have a dog as a sire for your puppies which at least is not gun-shy and is not hardmouthed, the latter being an hereditary defect very often.

Of course, some of the show champions work quite well but they have not actually proved themselves in public, although, if you particularly fancy a dog of this type, you can always go and view the dog and ask the owner to let you see it at work. It may not be in the shooting season, but you can get a very fair idea of how it will retrieve a dummy and ask the owner to fire a gun over the dog just to prove that he is not gun-shy. The theories attached to breeding winning dogs are endless. Many people have their own methods and their own ideas. There are the 'Rule of thumb' breeders—successful too—who seem to produce year after year good stock, and you have the theorists, the geneticists who say only by their methods can purity of line and production of certain points be obtained. Well, they may be correct—I don't know—but I think you will find it much more effective to contact a good, successful breeder who has produced the winners in practice and get their advice rather than buy an expensive book on genetics and try and follow out their theories, putting them into practice. It may be a rewarding job for you but it may possibly be highly disappointing. In any case, if you are relying simply on the book you have no-one in whom you can confide. When you are following the advice of the proved successful breeder you can always go back, confide in him, tell him your troubles and ask for further advice. In the Labrador fraternity you will always find someone ready and willing to give you every assistance in your breeding efforts.

CHAPTER 7

GENERAL MANAGEMENT

LET us turn for the moment to the question of kenneling. If you have in mind setting up a small kennel, the approach must of necessity be different from that of a person just wanting the odd companion dog. In this latter case he can, of course, live in the house, in the kitchen, or in the outhouse, and I suggest from the very first, give him his own corner, his own box, his own mat, and make him use it. He'll soon come to look on that as his own particular domain, and he'll not become a nuisance, wandering about the house, penetrating to the bedrooms, and otherwise disturbing the household generally. You can have him in the drawing room in the evening to sit before the fire for company, but when it's time to go to bed, just a word 'Back to your box', 'Back to your mat' and a well-trained dog should go happily and never be heard again until he comes to greet you when you come down in the morning.

However, if you wish to start a kennel, then, of course, it is advisable to start a sectional building in your paddock, or wherever you wish to place it. The modern kennels can be bought section at a time until you have eventually the whole range. Of course, if you can buy the thing outright to start with, so much the better, but a lot of people believe in walking before they run and so go to a good maker, get a first-class kennel, and tell him you want the type to which additions can be made as and when you wish to extend.

Situate the kennel facing south, if it's near a wind-break or a good wall, or a good stout hedge so much the better. Dogs will not stand damp and draught; get the kennel up off the damp floor if there is damp about, and above all, see there are no draughts. Give him an interior sleeping box with just enough space for him to go into. He likes a dark, cosy corner in which to spend the night. I can't emphasize this too much. Dogs naturally are hardy and they will withstand cold, but not damp nor draughts, and I suggest to you, however tired you are, when you bring your dog home after a long walk or a day's shooting, rub him down with a towel and dry him out as well as you can. Air him off before the fire if possible before you shut him up in his bed for the night.

These humane precautions will prolong the life of your dog and there's nothing more pitiable than a dog suffering from kennel lameness and rheumatism brought on by going into his bed wet through and steaming himself dry.

Most dog books, or rather books on dogs, contain a chapter or two on canine ailments. Many old breeders are diehards where treatment of their dogs is concerned, but the great progress in veterinary science, particularly since the war, has proved that many of these remedies were barely effective. Apart from the simple worming of the dog, I should strongly recommend if any misfortune should arise, that you consult a veterinary surgeon. I am not going to relate all the medicines and methods of treatment used in our pre-war kennel because I have seen such evidence of the improvement in drugs and their administration and of the knowledge acquired in research regarding these drugs, as applied to the dog, that I am convinced that only the qualified man is capable of advising and administering these drugs.

What I do strongly suggest is that by careful feeding, good kennels, and correct exercising, you maintain a healthy, happy dog, and if you have got your puppy or your brood bitch from a first-class kennel, where the foundation of good health has been previously laid for you, you need have no worries as to the future. Labradors are a very hardy breed, they are not susceptible to illness generally, and apart from accidents which can catch up with any animal, or human for that matter, there is little apart from emphasizing again reasonable treatment, and your dog should live a trouble-free life. Should he contract some ailment or should he meet with an accident, then I do strongly suggest you get in qualified advice, and as immediately as possible.

How many times in my experience have I come across a person whose one and only dog is suddenly taken ill, responding to the advice of some immediate neighbour; maybe well-meant but not really sound. The dog does not respond to treatment and is obviously flagging and you are forced eventually to call in the help of a veterinary surgeon. Now I do most strongly advise you not to be reticent in any respect. Tell him exactly the circumstances, why you didn't call him in the first place, what you have done in the meantime and how long the dog has been ill. Veterinary surgeons are understanding people and they will not hold it against you that you have inadvertently handicapped them in their fight to return your dog to health.

CHAPTER 8

SUMMING UP

OWNING a dog is not a complicated business. You may not know the first thing about dogs, but you'll soon learn; but be advised, do not take too seriously to heart the gratuitous advice handed out by odd types of people where dogs are concerned. They will give you specific instructions for one thing or another, but believe me, common sense treatment is important above all. If you have a young baby or a child, rear your puppy as you would your own off-spring. That is one of the easiest and most effective methods of dog management and rearing that I know. Resist at all times the unqualified advice; listen only to qualified advice through breed clubs, training clubs, and most important your fully qualified veterinary surgeon. In matters of general conduct of a kennel, you can always refer back to the person from whom you have bought your foundation stock; their interest will be genuine, they will not look on you as being in competition with them but will be pleased to help you throughout the time of your initiation until you can stand alone as an accredited breeder in your own right.

May I wish you every success with your Labrador and perhaps your future kennel and on behalf of all the Club members and the various Labrador Clubs in this country, I can extend to you a very hearty welcome, and let us hope you may be able to show your dog eventually. It must be registered, of course, with the Kennel Club and they will supply you a form and the breeder will supply you with a certificate and sign it. You pay your fee and then, after your dog is six months of age, you can show him in whatever class of show you wish, always providing they are run under Kennel Club rules. Never be tempted to show him at any show other than the official events. There are small member shows generally held on an afternoon or during the evening where you will find a lot more novices and you can exchange views, look at each others' dogs, and learning together, progress to the higher grade of open shows which are promoted in the towns and very often in conjunction with the Agricultural Show in your district. Here the entry fee and prize money are both higher and, presuming you have a fair amount of success, then you can try your dog out at one of the big championship shows and here again you double up your entry fee and also double up the prize money. We call them championship shows because all the judges at these shows have to be approved by the Kennel Club, and they have had to do a certain number of other shows to qualify them for these special events. The Kennel Club issue to these shows what are called Kennel Club Challenge Certificates, one for the best dog, one for the best bitch. If you are fortunate enough to win three of these awards for best dog or best bitch in your breed at three championship shows under three different judges, you can then call your dog a show champion. If your dog is fully trained to the gun you can then take it to a field trial and let it run in public for a working certificate which if granted will entitle you to call the dog champion.

Many a great kennel has been formed from a small beginning. May I say I hope, perhaps from your first baby puppy, you may progress so far on the road that you will be eventually received into that great body of breeders who provide the top competition at field trials and at the championship shows. Good puppy rearing and good showing.

LISTS OF CLUBS TO JOIN

LABRADOR CLUBS

The Labrador Retriever Club—Mr. C. Brown, 19 Dulverton Road, New Eltham, S.E.9.

Midland Counties Labrador Retriever Club—Mrs. H. Taylor, Chase Cliffe, Whatstandwell, Nr. Matlock.

The Labrador Club of Scotland—Mr. J. M. Manson, School House, Queen School, Dunfermline.

Northumberland and Durham Labrador Retriever Club—Mr. T. H. Hogg, School House, Ebchester, Corbett, Co. Durham.

Yellow Labrador Club—Mrs. A. Wormald, Glenstuart, Cummertrees, Annan.

The Three Ridings Labrador Club—Mr. C. H. Hawarth, Dale Close, St. John's Hill, Abberford, Nr. Leeds.

Labrador Retriever Club of Ulster—Mr. T. Lowry, 263 Castlereagh Road, Belfast.

RETRIEVER CLUBS

The Retriever Society (International Gun dog League)—Mr. E. Holland Buckley, 1-4 Clarges Street, Piccadilly, W.1.

United Retriever Club—Mrs. E. Saunders, School House, Queen Anne's School, Birmingham.

Eastern Counties Retriever Society—Mr. F. P. Busuttil, The Old Rectory, Swardeston, Norfolk.

Herts., Beds., Bucks., Berks. and Hants. Retriever Society—Mrs. J. Saunders, Liddly, Ashmansworth, Nr. Newbury, Berks.

Yorkshire Retriever Field Trial Society—Mr. R. F. Bilton, 149 High Street, Hull, Yorks.

DOG TRAINING CLUBS AND SOCIETIES REGISTERED AT THE KENNEL CLUB

By all means join a National Breed Club, but for the purpose of receiving instruction in the training of your dog I suggest you join a local society of which there are over a hundred in existence and the numbers are still growing. Here with other novices both you and the dog are trained together, this concerted training of course providing the best results. Write to the Secretary, The Kennel Club, 1–4 Clarges Street, Piccadilly. W.1, and ask him for the name and address of the Secretary of the Club nearest to your home. NOTE: State the breed of your dog, for some societies are confined to just one breed.